LIONEL MESSI

BY ERIN NICKS

WORLD'S **GREATEST** SOCCER PLAYERS

SportsZone

An Imprint of Abdo Publishing
abdobooks.com

abdobooks.com

Published by Abdo Publishing, a division of ABDO, PO Box 398166, Minneapolis, Minnesota 55439.

Printed in China
092019
012020

THIS BOOK CONTAINS RECYCLED MATERIALS

Cover Photo: Manu Fernandez/AP Images
Interior Photos: Daniel Ochoa de Olza/AP Images, 4, 6–7; Alterphotos/Sipa/AP Images, 8; Javier Heinzmann/Escuela General Las Heras/Latin Content WO/Getty Images, 10; Peter Schneider/Keystone/AP Images, 13; Victor R. Caivano/AP Images, 14; Manu Fernandez/AP Images, 16; Natacha Pisarenko/AP Images, 19; Giuliano Bevilacqua/Sipa USA/AP Images, 20–21; Sergio Torres/AP Images, 22; Julio Cortez/AP Images, 24, 27; Craig Mercer/Cal Sports Media/Zuma Wire/AP Images, 28

Editor: Patrick Donnelly
Series Designer: Craig Hinton

Library of Congress Control Number: 2019941993

Publisher's Cataloging-in-Publication Data

Names: Nicks, Erin, author.
Title: Lionel Messi / by Erin Nicks
Description: Minneapolis, Minnesota : Abdo Publishing, 2020 | Series: World's greatest soccer players | Includes online resources and index.
Identifiers: ISBN 9781532190636 (lib. bdg.) | ISBN 9781644943427 (pbk.) | ISBN 9781532176487 (ebook)
Subjects: LCSH: Messi, Lionel, 1987- --Juvenile literature. | Futbol Club Barcelona--Juvenile literature. | European football--Biography--Juvenile literature. | Soccer players--Biography--Juvenile literature. | Professional athletes--Biography--Juvenile literature.
Classification: DDC 796.3340922--dc23

TABLE OF CONTENTS

QATAR
AIRWAYS
10

CHAPTER
ONE

THE PERFECT NIGHT

Lionel Messi called April 23, 2017, a perfect night of soccer. Messi's club, FC Barcelona, was facing Real Madrid at the Bernabeu, their archrival's home stadium. Barcelona needed a win to close the gap on Real Madrid for first place in La Liga, Spain's top league.

However, the game started rough for the star. After taking an elbow to the face, Messi played much of the game with a blood-soaked rag in his mouth. That didn't stop him from scoring a goal. But with the match tied 2–2 and time running out, he knew one goal wasn't enough.

Lionel Messi, *right*, fights off a challenge from Real Madrid's Gareth Bale on April 23, 2017.

In the final minute of the match, Barcelona went on the attack. Sergi Roberto sprinted up the center of the field with the ball. He passed to Jordi Alba, who took the ball out wide left, looking for Messi. It was a move Alba and Messi had practiced in the past. Messi ran to the edge of the penalty area, waiting for the ball. Alba flicked a pass to Messi, who rocketed the ball past goalkeeper Keylor Navas and into the bottom left corner of the Real Madrid net.

The Real Madrid supporters were stunned. Messi ran up the field, peeled off his jersey, and held it out in front of his chest to show the fans. Not only had the goal kept Barcelona's title hopes alive, but it was also the 500th goal Messi had scored for the famous club.

Messi is fouled by Real Madrid's Sergio Ramos, *bottom*, in the always contentious *El Clasico* match.

QATAR
AIRWAYS
Fly
Emirates
Emirates
RMCF

Messi celebrates his huge goal against Real Madrid.

Messi is one of the most celebrated soccer players in the world. Through 2018 he'd already won the Ballon d'Or trophy—given to the world's best player—five times.

That matched Cristiano Ronaldo for the most ever. He also won a record sixth Golden Shoe award as the leading scorer among all European club players in 2018–19.

That individual success has led to great results for Barcelona, the only professional team Messi ever played for. Through 2019 he'd helped the club win nine La Liga titles, four Champions League titles, and six Copas Del Rey. Messi also led his Argentina national team to the gold medal at the 2008 Olympics in Beijing and to the final of the 2014 World Cup in Brazil.

LA PULGA

At 5 feet 7 inches (1.7 m), Messi is a smaller player who pesters the opposing team with his dribbling and defense. That's why his nickname is La Pulga, which is Spanish for "the Flea."

Despite offers from other clubs, Messi stayed in Barcelona, where he broke records while thrilling fans all over the planet. Not bad for an undersized player who had to cross oceans as a boy for a chance to grow up a soccer star.

CHAPTER
TWO

ARGENTINA'S **SHINING STAR**

Lionel Andrés Messi was born June 24, 1987, in Rosario, Argentina. Even from a young age, Lionel was a talented soccer player. However, he was much smaller than the other kids his age. And by age 11, he didn't seem to be catching up to them. So a doctor prescribed growth hormones to help his body develop faster.

But the medicine was expensive, and Lionel's family couldn't afford to pay for it. FC Barcelona was already scouting Lionel. Club management agreed to cover his medical costs if he signed a contract with them.

Messi, shown at age 5, was small compared to his peers.

So in 2000, Lionel moved overseas with his father and joined Barcelona's academy. Lionel started playing for Barcelona's under-14 team. By 2004 he had been called up to Barcelona's senior team. At 17 years old, he was the youngest player in La Liga.

Messi quickly showed that Barcelona had made a good investment. He became known for his quickness and accuracy while attacking with a left-footed shot. And with his individual progress came unmatched team success.

In 2005–06 Messi played a big role as Barcelona won the Champions League—a season-long competition that determines the best club team in Europe—for the first time in 14 years. Three seasons later Barcelona captured its first European treble. The club won La Liga, the Champions League title, and the Copa Del Rey.

Messi quickly moved up to Barcelona's senior team and had an immediate impact.

10

Messi, *left*, and Xavi celebrate a goal during their rout of Real Madrid in 2009.

Few matches are as important to Barcelona fans as *El Clasico*. That's what they call any match against Real Madrid. Early in his career, Messi thrived against

Barcelona's top rival. That showed in one meeting late in the 2008–09 season. In the 35th minute, after a slick takeaway by teammate Xavi, Messi easily walked the ball up and sent a low kick into the corner of the Madrid net. His second strike came exactly 40 minutes later, again with help from Xavi. After fighting off defenders, Xavi flicked the ball up to Messi. With a quick kick from his left foot, Messi sent the ball past the goalkeeper and into the net, and Barcelona was on its way to a 6–2 rout.

LANDSLIDE VICTORY

The winner of the Ballon d'Or is decided by a poll of soccer journalists all over the world. Messi's first Ballon d'Or was close to a unanimous decision —he received 473 points out of a possible 480.

Messi capped an excellent 2009 by winning his first Ballon d'Or in December. It was the start of an incredible streak for him and his club. By 2011 he had won three Champions League titles, five La Liga titles, and three Ballon d'Or trophies, in addition to playing in two World Cups for Argentina. As amazing as it sounds, Messi was just getting started.

Qatar
Foundation

CHAPTER
THREE

MASTERFUL MESSI

Lionel Messi made 2012 a year to remember. He was only 24 when he became Barcelona's all-time leading scorer in all competitions with his 234th career goal in March 2012. He went on to score 73 goals in all competitions for Barcelona in the 2011–12 season, breaking the record for the most goals scored in one season by a European club player.

But he was far from finished. In December 2012 Messi scored his 91st and final goal of the calendar year, counting all competitions for Barcelona and Argentina's

Messi shows off the Ballon d'Or trophy to Barcelona fans in January 2012. He was about to go on a record scoring binge that would earn him his fourth Ballon d'Or.

national team. That total shattered the previous record of 85, set in 1972 by Gerd Müller, who played for Bayern Munich and West Germany. In 2012 Messi also became the first player to win a fourth Ballon d'Or trophy. He scored 46 goals in the 2012–13 season, the most in the Spanish league, and Barcelona took home its sixth La Liga title in Messi's eight seasons.

There was one big honor Messi hadn't yet claimed, though. In 2014 he led Argentina into the World Cup. It was Messi's third time in the tournament, and he was determined to lead his country to its first world title since 1986. Messi scored four goals in the tournament, and Argentina got all the way to the final. However, they fell to Germany in extra time. Still, Messi's performance earned him the Golden Ball as the World Cup's top player.

Messi was brilliant in the 2014 World Cup, but Argentina came up short, losing to Germany 1–0 in the final.

The records kept piling up. The night of November 22, 2014, was a magical one for Messi. He put all his unique skills on display to dominate a league match with Seville. First he scored off a free kick, a wicked strike that bent in the air and sailed past the leaping goalkeeper.

Then in the 72nd minute, Messi showed his willingness to fight for every goal. He managed to redirect a cross from teammate Neymar while sliding into the net to score his second goal of the match.

Six minutes later, Messi struck again. This time he used his legendary dribbling skills to dodge multiple defenders before rocketing a shot from the edge of the penalty area into the net. Barcelona won the match 5–1, and Messi's hat trick made

Messi's teammates toss him in the air as they celebrate his record-setting night on November 22, 2014.

BARÇA
BARÇA
21
beko

LFP
10

him La Liga's all-time leading scorer with 253 goals in league matches.

Messi continued to show that he could dominate a game in many ways. His shooting, dribbling, and passing skills all put him among the greatest players to ever step onto the field. And his club team kept piling up victories. But success on the international stage remained elusive, and his frustrations would soon boil over.

CAPTAIN MESSI

Messi was named Barcelona's captain at the start of the 2018–19 season, replacing Andrés Iniesta.

Messi's unique ability to control the ball helps him create scoring opportunities.

CHAPTER
FOUR

BARCELONA *SÍ*, ARGENTINA *NO*

One of Lionel Messi's most memorable goals during the 2014–15 season came against Athletic Bilbao. He dipped and curled the ball around three opponents on the right wing before sprinting to the net. Once inside the box, he faked out a defender and sent the ball flying past the goalkeeper. Barcelona won another European treble that year, taking home titles in La Liga, the Copa del Rey, and the Champions League.

Yet outside of the Olympics, his efforts to lead his national team to victory proved fruitless. Argentina

Messi reacts to missing a penalty kick in a shootout loss to Chile in the final of the Copa America Centenario.

stormed through the competition to reach the final of the Copa America Centenario, a 2016 tournament that featured the top national teams in South America and North America. However, after a scoreless 120 minutes in the final, Chile won a 4–2 shootout to claim the title.

A devastated Messi—who had missed his attempt in the shootout—said he was done playing for Argentina in international competitions. "For me, the national team is over," said Messi, who was 29 at the time. "I've done all I can. It hurts not to be a champion."

He eventually reconsidered his decision and helped Argentina qualify for the 2018 World Cup. But the team was in disarray. Messi played well, but he didn't get much help from his teammates. Argentina fell to eventual champion France 4–3 in the round of 16. The next year, they lost to Brazil in the semifinals of the Copa America,

Messi struggled for answers in the wake of Argentina's loss to Chile.

COPA AMERICA
USA 2016
adizero

MESSI
10
unicef

extending Argentina's trophy drought.

As disappointing as his international career had been, Messi continued to win trophies and awards in Spain. He again captured the Copa del Rey with Barcelona in 2016–17, finishing the season with 54 goals and his fourth Golden Shoe. In 2017–18, Barcelona won a La Liga/Copa del Rey double—the third of Messi's career—and he won his fifth Golden Shoe. And in February 2019 he scored his 50th hat trick and his 650th career goal. He proved himself to be one of the greatest scorers of all time and has led Barcelona to its most successful era in club history.

GIVING BACK

Messi established a charitable foundation in 2007 to help children in need. His foundation has funded centers and medical treatment for children in Argentina, Spain, and throughout the world. And in 2017 he helped build 20 classrooms for children in Syria, allowing 1,600 children to return to their lessons in a country badly affected by war.

The cheers of Barcelona fans wash over Messi as he celebrates a goal in a Champions League match in April 2019.

GLOSSARY

academy
A program run by a club to train young players and help them improve their skills.

cross
A pass delivered from the side of the field toward the middle.

flick
A short kick.

free kick
An unguarded kick awarded to a team after a foul.

hat trick
Three goals by the same player in one game.

penalty area
The box in front of the goal where a player is granted a penalty kick if he or she is fouled in it.

treble
Winning three major competitions in a single season.

World Cup
The biggest soccer tournament in the world, held once every four years among national teams.

MORE INFORMATION

BOOKS

Bader, Bonnie. *What Is the World Cup?* New York: Penguin Workshop, 2018.

Billioud, Jean-Michel. *Soccer Stars: Meet 40 Game Changers*. London: Wide-Eyed Editions, 2018.

Part, Michael. *The Flea: The Amazing Story of Leo Messi*. Beverly Hills, CA: Sole Books, 2017.

ONLINE RESOURCES

Booklinks
NONFICTION NETWORK
FREE! ONLINE NONFICTION RESOURCES

To learn more about Lionel Messi, please visit **abdobooklinks.com** or scan this QR code. These links are routinely monitored and updated to provide the most current information available.

INDEX

ABOUT THE AUTHOR

Erin Nicks is from Thunder Bay, Ontario. She has written about sports for newspapers and websites for the past 20 years. She currently lives in Ottawa, Ontario.